GERMANY

Cath Senker

Photographs by Christof Schürpf

CHERRYTREE BOOKS

LETTERS FROM AROUND THE WORLD

Titles in this series

AUSTRALIA • BANGLADESH • BRAZIL • CANADA • CHINA • COSTA RICA
EGYPT • FRANCE • GERMANY • GREECE • INDIA • INDONESIA • ITALY
JAMAICA • JAPAN • KENYA • MEXICO • PAKISTAN • SOUTH AFRICA • SPAIN

A Cherrytree Book

Conceived and produced by

Nutshell
MEDIA

Intergen House
65-67 Western Road
Hove BN3 2JQ, UK
www.nutshellmedialtd.co.uk

First published in 2005 by
Evans Brothers Ltd
2A Portman Mansions
Chiltern Street
London W1U 6NR

Editor: Polly Goodman
Design: Mayer Media Ltd
Map artwork: Encompass Graphics Ltd
All other artwork: Mayer Media Ltd

All photographs were taken by Christof Schürpf.

Acknowledgements
The photographer would like to thank the Böhm family,
the staff and pupils of Turnseeschule, Freiburg,
Staatsweingut Blankenhornsberg, the University of
Freiburg and the Islamic Centre of Freiburg for all their
help with this book.

British Library Cataloguing in Publication Data
Senker, Cath
   Germany. – (Letters from around the world)
   1. Germany – Social conditions – 1990 – Juvenile
   literature
   2. Germany – Social life and customs – 21st century –
   Juvenile literature
   I. Title
943'.0882

ISBN 1 84234 277 0

Cover: Paul and two of his neighbours, Anna and Lukas,
standing in front of the Münster cathedral, the most
famous building in Freiburg.
Title page: Paul and his friends, Julius and Benjamin,
in their football club kit on the soccer field near Paul's
home.
This page: A vineyard near Ihringen, about 25 km
from Freiburg.
Contents page: Paul in summer clothes.
Glossary page: Paul on his bike with his sister Carla.
Further Information page: Paul with his friends in the
football team.
Index: The German flag flying from a boat on the Rhine.

Contents

My Country

Saturday, 25 September

Scheffelstrasse 84
3rd floor
71903 Freiburg
Germany

Dear Kerry,

Hallo! (In German, this means the same as it does in English.)

My name is Paul Böhm (pronounced 'Powl Berm'). I'm eight years old and I live in Freiburg im Breisgau (pronounced 'Fry-borg im Brize-gow'), a city in south-west Germany. I live with my mum, dad and my sister Carla, who's 14.

I'm learning English, so it's great to practise with a real English person!

Write back soon!

From
Paul

Here I am in the back garden with my mum, Gabi, my dad, Thomas, and Carla. ➜

Germany is in Western Europe. In 1945, after the Second World War, it was divided into two: East Germany and West Germany. In 1990, the country became one again.

Germany's place in the world.

Germany shares borders with nine countries and has coastlines with two seas, the Baltic Sea and the North Sea.

Freiburg im Breisgau (Freiburg for short) is close to the borders with France and Switzerland. It is an important centre for trade in timber (wood) and wine. Goods can be brought in and sent to other countries by motorway (the *Autobahn*), rail and air.

Freiburg is an eco-city, which means its people try to protect the environment. Some industries run on solar power. Others make solar products, such as solar panels to heat water.

A view over Freiburg, with the Vosges mountains in France in the distance. Most of the city was rebuilt after it was bombed in the Second World War, so there are many modern buildings.

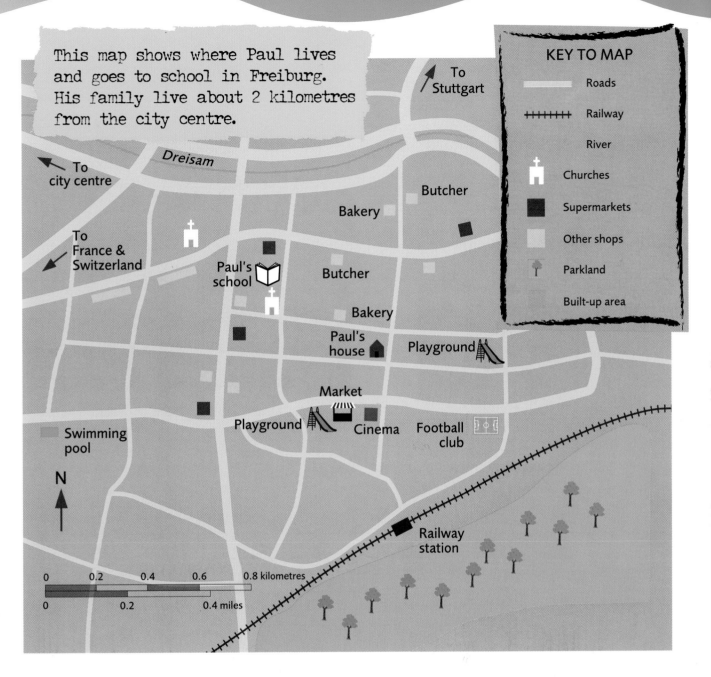

This map shows where Paul lives and goes to school in Freiburg. His family live about 2 kilometres from the city centre.

To Stuttgart

KEY TO MAP

Roads

Railway

River

Churches

Supermarkets

Other shops

Parkland

Built-up area

Dreisam

To city centre

To France & Switzerland

Butcher

Bakery

Paul's school

Butcher

Bakery

Paul's house

Playground

Market

Playground

Cinema

Football club

Swimming pool

N

Railway station

0   0.2   0.4   0.6   0.8 kilometres

0   0.2   0.4 miles

Freiburg has a university, a cathedral and several other interesting historical buildings. Many tourists visit the city and businesses hold conferences there.

The Dreisam river runs through the city on its way to the Rhine, Germany's main river. The Rhine is about 15 kilometres away from Freiburg.

Landscape and Weather

Freiburg is near the Black Forest, a mountain region covered in forests. Further east there are high mountains, called the Bavarian Alps. In the north there are low, flat plains.

The climate around Freiburg is mild and warm, perfect for growing grapes to make wine.

It rarely gets very hot or very cold in Germany. Winters are mild in the north, where the land is low. In the high Bavarian Alps, the winters are colder and it often snows.

The Rhine river begins in Switzerland. It runs through Germany and the Netherlands, before reaching the North Sea.

Freiburg's Climate

January
Temperature
4°C

61mm
Rainfall

July
Temperature
24°C

106mm
Rainfall

At Home

Like many people living in Germany's cities, Paul and his family live in a flat. It is on the third floor of a large house. There are three other flats in the house, one on each floor.

Paul and Carla in front of their house. They play here in their neighbours' back yard with friends.

The family watch TV,
listen to the stereo and
read in the living room.

Paul has lots of toy
cars and trucks, and
his own CD player.

In the flat there are three
bedrooms, a living room,
kitchen, bathroom and toilet.
There is a large hallway where
the family keep their piano.

Paul's bedroom has a high bed
with a special slide so he can
get up quickly in the morning!
Paul has a desk in his room
where he does his homework.

Paul brushes his teeth every morning and evening with his electric toothbrush.

Paul's flat has two balconies. They are used for hanging out washing, growing plants or for sitting in the sunshine. There is a back garden, too, which is shared with people in the other flats.

Paul is watering the plants on the balcony. Freiburg gets plenty of sunshine, so it's easy to grow flowers.

Saturday, 23 October

Scheffelstrasse 84
3rd floor
71903 Freiburg
Germany

Hallo Kerry,

Wie geht's? (You say 'Vee-gates'. That's German for 'How are you?')

Thanks for your letter. I've got a pet rabbit, too. His name's Ronja. I give him hay to eat and brush his fur to keep him clean. Ronja's hutch is in the garden and every week I clean it out. I let him run around in the garden but I can't leave him out in case he eats the plants. It's important to take care of the garden because we share it with the people in the other flats.

Bye for now.

From

Paul

↗

Here I am with Ronja in the back garden.

Food and Mealtimes

Most mornings, Paul has a bowl of muesli for breakfast, followed by a roll with butter and jam. Sometimes he has a boiled egg.

At the weekend, the family usually eat breakfast together. On weekdays, they help themselves to breakfast as soon as they get up. Paul's dad has usually eaten his breakfast and left for work by the time Paul gets up.

Paul and Carla have an egg, cereal and rolls for breakfast. German adults and older children usually drink coffee with their breakfast.

On summer weekends, the family barbecue sausages and eat their meals in the garden.

Carla and Paul have lunch with their mother at home. They usually eat a small lunch of pasta and salad.

The family eat dinner together between 6 and 8 p.m. They usually have noodles, pasta or a rice dish with vegetables or salad. Most German people have meat with their main meal, but Paul's family don't have meat every day.

Paul's mum prepares a salad with fresh basil grown on the balcony.

Paul's family walk to the local butcher's and bakery for fresh meat and bread, and buy fruit and vegetables at the outdoor market. Gabi grows herbs on one of the balconies, and tomatoes in the garden. She drives to the supermarket for the main shopping.

There are many different kinds of summer fruit at the outdoor market.

Friday, 19 November

Scheffelstrasse 84
3rd floor
71903 Freiburg
Germany

Hi Kerry,

Here's a recipe for *kartoffelpuffer*, or potato pancakes:

You will need: 6 medium potatoes, peeled and grated; 1 onion, grated; 2 eggs; $1/2$ teaspoon salt; pepper; 4 tablespoons flour; 1 teaspoon parsley; 2 tablespoons cooking oil.

1. Mix the potatoes with the eggs, flour, onion, parsley, salt and pepper.
2. Heat the oil in a frying pan and add 3 tablespoons of the mixture. This will make one pancake.
3. Spread the mixture evenly and fry on both sides until golden brown. Now make the other pancakes in the same way.

Guten Appetit! (This means 'Enjoy your food!')

Paul

Here are the potato pancakes I made with my mum. We ate them with apple sauce – delicious! ➤

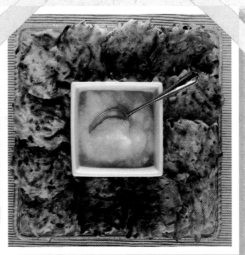

School Day

Every school morning, Paul leaves the house at 8.30 a.m. It takes him 10 minutes to walk to school, which is half a kilometre away.

Lessons start at 8.40 a.m and finish at 1 p.m. At 10.15 a.m there is a half-hour break, when the children can play games in the playground.

Paul started school when he was 6 years old. When he is 10, he will go to the secondary school next door.

Paul arrives at school with his friend Luca. Like most German schools, there is no uniform.

Paul studies geography, German, maths, RE, art and sport. The teachers use lots of games to make sure that learning is always fun.

There are two school terms a year in Germany, from September to February, and from February to July. The main holidays are the six-week summer holiday and two weeks at Christmas.

Every hour, Paul's class have a five-minute break and a stretch to keep them fresh and awake for their lessons.

Paul's class are making an ocean display in their art lesson. Paul cuts out a fish he has drawn to add it to the display.

Even though Paul only goes to school in the morning, he does lots of activities after school. He is a member of a football club that practises once a week after school. Every Monday afternoon he has a piano lesson.

Paul jumps over the boxes in PE.

Paul has his weekly piano lesson at his teacher's flat. Lots of children in Germany learn musical instruments.

Monday, 17 January

Scheffelstrasse 84
3rd floor
71903 Freiburg
Germany

Hi Kerry,

I'm glad the potato pancake recipe worked. It's delicious, isn't it? Today at school we had maths, art and PE. I love maths. Our teacher, Frau Ernst, makes it really good fun. She tells us a story and then gives us maths questions. I always work them out quickly! I also love football. I play at break time and after school in a football club.

What's your school like? Write back and tell me.

Tschüss! (Pronounced 'Choos'. This means 'Bye!')

Paul

In the maths lesson, our teacher called out the number seven and we had to get into groups of seven.

Off to Work

Paul's dad is a doctor. He works in a hospital in Offenburg, a city 60 kilometres away from Freiburg. He takes the train there every day. Paul's mum is a physiotherapist. She helps children to learn to move their bodies properly. She drives to work at a nursery.

Here is Paul's mum at work, helping a girl to improve her balance.

Many people in Freiburg work in modern industries such as IT, biotechnology and solar industries. Many others work in service industries, for example, running Freiburg's very good transport system.

In the countryside around Freiburg, there are many jobs in vineyards, picking grapes and making wine.

Free Time

Germans have up to six weeks' holiday every year, as well as weekends off. People spend their free time at sports centres, theatres, cinemas, libraries or campsites.

Football is the most popular sport. Most Germans belong to a sports club or other type of club to do their favourite pastime.

Paul is the goalkeeper in his football team. Here he is playing in a school tournament. His team won third place.

There are four indoor pools and three outdoor pools in Freiburg, as well as a learners' pool.

Paul loves football, cycling, swimming and reading. At the weekend, the family go to the park or swimming pool, or for a bike ride. In the summer, they often rent a house in Italy, France or Switzerland and spend a few weeks there with friends.

Paul and his friends have turned a table upside down so they can play with their spinning toys.

Religion

Two thirds of the people in Germany are Christians. There are also about 3 million Muslims, and some Buddhists and Hindus. Nearly a third of the people do not follow any religion. The biggest Christian festivals are Christmas, Carnival (in February), Easter and Whitsun.

Paul lights a candle in the cathedral and prays for a family friend who is ill.

This Muslim boy is praying at the mosque in the Islamic centre in Freiburg.

Tuesday, 8 February

Scheffelstrasse 84
3rd floor
71903 Freiburg
Germany

Hi Kerry,

It was amazing here last week because it was Carnival (we spell it *Karneval* in German). Carnival is a time for having fun before the serious time of Lent. On Thursday, we wore fancy dress and joined the crowds in the city centre. There were food and drink stalls everywhere, and people were dancing in the streets. All weekend there were celebrations. On Monday it was the final procession with carnival groups from all around Freiburg.

Do you have any carnivals?
Write back and tell me.

Tschüss!

Paul

Here I am with Carla – we've dressed up in fancy dress for Carnival.

Fact File

Flag: Black, red and gold became Germany's national colours in the nineteenth century. Different flags were used in the early twentieth century. In 1949, West Germany adopted the flag below. After Germany became one again, this became the flag of the whole country.

Capital city: Berlin is the capital of Germany. When Germany was divided into two countries, Berlin was divided too. After Germany became one country again in 1990, Berlin became its capital.

Other major cities: Hamburg, Munich, Cologne, Frankfurt and Essen.

Population: Over 82 million. Germany has the largest population in Europe.

Size: 357,021 km².

Language: German.

Currency: The euro (€), which is divided into cents. There are 100 cents in a euro.

Famous buildings: Germany has large Roman Catholic cathedrals, including the Dom in Cologne, the Münster in Freiburg (above) and the Frauenkirche in Munich. It is famous for its castles, especially the Royal Castles in the Bavarian mountains.

Main religions: 68 per cent of Germans are Christians. About 3.7 per cent are Muslims. There are also Orthodox Christians, and some Hindus, Buddhists and Jews. Around 28 per cent of Germans do not practise any religion.

Main industries: Iron, steel, coal, cement, chemicals, machinery, vehicles, electronics, food and drink, shipbuilding, textiles.

Famous people: Germany is famous for its composers, thinkers and scientists from the past, such as the composer Johannes Brahms (1833–1897) and the scientist Albert Einstein (1879–1955). Adolf Hitler was Germany's brutal leader from 1933–1945. Marlene Dietrich (1901–1992) is the best-known German actress.

Highest mountain: Zugspitze (2,962 m), in the Bavarian Alps.

Longest river: The Rhine (1,390 km) flows from the Alps in Switzerland north and west through Germany. It has many old and famous cities along its banks. There are also industrial cities that pollute the waters.

Stamps: Stamps in Germany show famous people from the past, important events, buildings, plants and animals.

29

Glossary

biotechnology Using living cells for industrial and scientific work.

carnival A big festival in many Christian countries just before Lent, with music, dancing and food.

cathedral The main church in an area.

Lent The season of forty days before Easter when Christians think about things they have done wrong.

medical research The study of ways to improve medicines.

Orthodox Christians Members of Eastern Churches, such as the Greek and Russian Church.

physiotherapist A person who teaches people exercises to strengthen their bodies.

plains A large area of flat ground.

Second World War A major war that was fought from 1939 to 1945. The USA, Russia, Britain, France and other countries defeated Germany, Italy and Japan.

service industries Businesses that serve people rather than making goods, such as hospitals, tourism and transport.

solar Using the sun's energy.

tournament A sports competition with different teams, which leave the competition when they lose. At the end, there is one winning team.

vineyard A piece of land where grapes are grown for making wine.

Further Information

Information books:

Changing Face of Germany by Sonja Schanz (Hodder Wayland, 2002)

Country Topics: Germany by Ting Morris, Rachel Wright and Teri Gower (Franklin Watts, 2003)

Countrywise: Germany and German by Janine Amos (Chrysalis, 2003)

Fiesta!: Germany by Tessa Paul (Franklin Watts, 2001)

Picture a Country: Germany by Henry Pluckrose (Franklin Watts, 2001)

A River Journey: The Rhine by Ronan Foley (Hodder Children's Books, 2003)

Take Your Camera to Germany by Ted Park (Raintree, 2003)

A Visit to Germany by Peter Roop (Heinemann, 2000)

We Come From Germany by Mike Hirst (Hodder Wayland, 2001)

World of Recipes: Germany by Sue Townsend (Heinemann, 2003)

Websites:

German Culture
www.germanculture.com.ua/
Facts, history, recipes and tips.

CIA Factbook
www.cia.gov/cia/publications/factbook/
Facts and figures about Germany and other countries.

Germany for Kids
www.germany-info.org/
Use the search engine on this site to find out all about home, school, music, food, free time and religion

Songs in German
www.songsforteaching.com/germansongs.htm
Read the words and hear the music for some German songs.

Index